REMARKABLE
PEOPLE

Danica
Patrick

by Laura Pratt

www.av2books.com

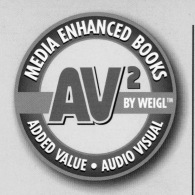

AV² provides enriched content that supplements and complements this book. Weigl's AV² books strive to create inspired learning and engage young minds in a total learning experience.

Your AV² Media Enhanced books come alive with...

Audio
Listen to sections of the book read aloud.

Key Words
Study vocabulary, and complete a matching word activity.

Video
Watch informative video clips.

Quizzes
Test your knowledge.

Embedded Weblinks
Gain additional information for research.

Slide Show
View images and captions, and prepare a presentation.

Try This!
Complete activities and hands-on experiments.

... and much, much more!

Go to **www.av2books.com**, and enter this book's unique code.

BOOK CODE

P 1 1 0 1 5 1

AV² by Weigl brings you media enhanced books that support active learning.

Published by AV² by Weigl
350 5th Avenue, 59th Floor
New York, NY 10118

www.av2books.com   www.weigl.com

Library of Congress Cataloging-in-Publication Data

Pratt, Laura.
  Danica Patrick / Laura Pratt.
     p. cm. -- (Remarkable people)
  Includes index.
  ISBN 978-1-61913-534-5 (hardcover : alk. paper) -- ISBN 978-1-61913-589-5 (softcover : alk. paper)
  1. Patrick, Danica, 1982---Juvenile literature. 2. Automobile racing drivers--United States--Biography--Juvenile literature.
  3. Women automobile racing drivers--United States--Biography--Juvenile literature. I. Title.
  GV1032.P38P73 2013
  796.72092--dc23
  [B]
                             2012000947

Printed in the United States of America in North Mankato, Minnesota
1 2 3 4 5 6 7 8 9 0 16 15 14 13 12

WEP170512
062012

Senior Editor: Heather Kissock
Art Director: Terry Paulhus

Photograph Credits
Weigl acknowledges Getty Images as the primary image supplier for this title. Every reasonable effort has been made to trace ownership and to obtain permission to reprint copyright material. The publishers would be pleased to have any errors or omissions brought to their attention so that they may be corrected in subsequent printings.

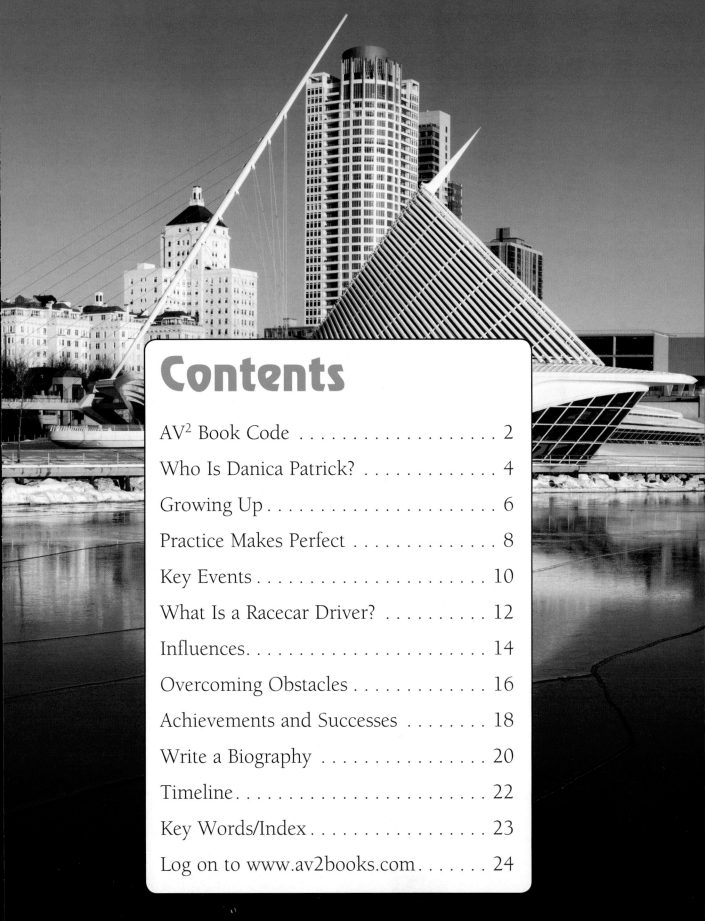

Contents

Who Is Danica Patrick?

Danica Patrick is one of the most famous female racecar drivers in North America. Danica races in the **NASCAR series**. She spent the first part of her career racing in the **IndyCar** series. Danica began racing **professionally** in 2005. Since then, she has taken part in more than 100 races.

Racecar driving is a sport that is dominated by men. Danica has attracted attention because she is one of the few women in this field. She has won awards and earned recognition for her skills on the racetrack.

"I don't feel like there's anything that I need to do for anybody else. I want to win bad enough for myself anyway, that nothing anybody can say can make me want to win any more."

Danica's success has put her in demand in other fields as well. She often works as a model and has appeared in *Sports Illustrated* as well as several fashion magazines. She is also a spokesperson for a variety of products. Danica has taken on minor acting roles on several television programs, including *CSI: Crime Scene Investigation*.

Growing Up

Danica Sue Patrick was born on March 25, 1982, in Beloit, Wisconsin. She grew up in nearby Roscoe, Illinois, with her parents, T.J. and Bev, and her younger sister, Brooke. T.J. and Bev were small business owners. They have sold a variety of products, ranging from coffee to plate glass.

Danica and her sister were around racing from an early age. This is because T.J. used to race snowmobiles, **motocross** bikes, and midget cars in his spare time. Danica began racing go-karts when she was 10 years old. However, it was Brooke who first expressed an interest in charging around the track in a go-kart. In 1992, when she was eight years old, Brooke crashed her kart three times. She decided go-karting was not the sport for her. Danica took over her sister's kart and never looked back.

■ Today, Danica's parents are two of her most loyal supporters. They often show up at races to cheer her on.

Get to Know Wisconsin

FLOWER
Wood Violet

TREE
Sugar Maple

BIRD
Robin

Wisconsin is nicknamed the Badger State. Early miners in the state often dug homes or tunnels out of hillsides, like badgers.

Noah's Ark, the largest waterpark in the United States, is located in Wisconsin Dells. It has 51 water rides and two giant wave pools.

More than 600 types of cheese are made in Wisconsin, including Swiss, cheddar, colby, and Gouda.

Wisconsin's capital city is Madison. It became the capital in 1836.

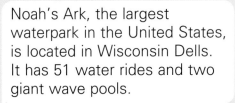

Think about it!

Danica's early interest in racecars is not considered typical for a girl. Many people questioned her desire to race cars. She pursued racing anyway and experienced success quickly. What kind of personality traits do you think someone must have to continue something when others doubt them?

Practice Makes Perfect

In her first go-kart race, Danica was **lapped** by the competition within six runs around the track. She realized then how important concentration and determination would be in improving her performance. By the end of the season, Danica finished second in her age group. The next year, she placed second in her region and fourth in the national Yamaha Sportsman class. Danica continued to hone her skills. In 1994, she won her first World Karting Association national championship. Danica would go on to win other regional and national titles.

When Danica was 16, she made the switch from go-karts to **open-wheeled** cars. She then traveled to England to compete in the Formula Vauxhall Winter Series. Danica finished the series in ninth position. She advanced to the British Zetek Formula Ford Series the following season. When Danica finished second at Brands Hatch, a popular racing circuit in England, hers was the best performance ever by an American in the history of the event.

■ Many future racecar drivers get their start racing go-karts.

In 1997, Danica had caught the attention of Indy 500 winner Bobby Rahal. Bobby was **scouting** young drivers for the Jaguar Formula 1 team he managed. Shortly after Danica returned to the United States in 2001, Bobby signed her to a **development deal** with his Rahal Letterman Racing IndyCar team.

Bobby Rahal provided the funding needed to get Danica's racing career moving. He was also one of her key advisors.

Key Events

In 2005, Danica made the switch from amateur to professional racing. In May of that year, she became the fourth woman ever to race in the Indianapolis 500. She started in the fourth position. This was the highest start any woman had ever achieved at that race. Danica broke another record by becoming the first woman to lead a race in the Indianapolis 500. She was unable to maintain her lead, however, and finished in fourth place. This was the best finish for a woman at the Indy 500. She was named the Indianapolis 500 **Rookie** of the Year for her performance in the race.

In 2007, Danica began driving for the Andretti Autosport Team. The next year, she won the Indy Japan 300. This win made her the first woman to win an Indy race anywhere. In 2009, she surpassed her fourth-place finish at the Indy 500 by placing third.

■ The 2008 Japan Indy 300 was Danica's 50th race as an IndyCar driver.

Thoughts from Danica

Danica is passionate about racing cars. Here are some of the comments she has made about driving fast cars and living the life of a racecar driver.

Danica talks about her approach to racing.

"I feel like, sometimes, people, because of the amount of media, because of the amount of attention, people seem to think I have to do things. Like, I have to win right now! But I don't feel like that."

Danica comments on the risks of driving fast cars.

"You're at risk being in your own house. ...There's a chance for tragedy every second."

Danica talks about how she drives when she is not racing.

"I don't like to drive at enormous top speed, but I do like to drive a little bit faster than everyone else. So if everybody on the highway is doing 80, I'll do 82 or something, and if people are driving 60, I'll want to do 62. I think there's something in my blood, in my instincts, that makes me want to overtake."

Danica explains how she deals with the expectations placed on her.

"I never get frustrated with expectations from everyone else. I just know I go out there and give everything I have, and if that's not good enough, then it's not good enough."

Danica describes how she feels about being a role model.

"I'm not...trying to be a role model. I haven't tried to go out of my way to inspire people. When you're real and you're authentic and you try to give honest answers all the time, then it's easy."

Danica looks back on her career.

"It's just my story...and the lessons that I learned along the way and that it wasn't all a peachy keen, wonderful life. It was hard, and probably, when I look back on it, it's harder looking back than in the moment."

What Is a Racecar Driver?

Racecar driving is a very exciting sport. Drivers compete against each other to see who can make it around the track fastest. It is one of the most popular sports to watch on television.

There are several different types of car racing. Each has different rules, cars, and tracks. Some of the more common types of car racing are **Formula One** racing, **drag racing**, and stock car racing. Sometimes, races take place on tracks that are just used for the race. These are called closed-course races. Other times, races take place on regular roads that are closed to other cars during the event. This is called street racing.

Racecar drivers have to be physically strong and have a good level of fitness. In order to work around the traffic on the course at a high speed, they also need to have an excellent sense of **precision**. It also helps to have good reflexes and vision.

■ A stock car looks similar to cars found in driveways across the country. They are fitted, however, with equipment that makes them true racing cars.

Racecar Drivers 101

Janet Guthrie (1938–)

Janet Guthrie was born in Iowa City, Iowa, but moved to Florida with her family when she was three years old. After graduating from the University of Michigan in 1960, Janet became a space engineer. In her spare time, she liked to race cars. In 1977, Janet qualified to start at the Daytona 500. She was the first woman to earn a spot in the cup series. In the same season, Janet raced in the Indy 500. The following year, Janet finished ninth at the Indy 500 and won $84,000. Janet had her best finish at the Milwaukee 200, taking fifth place. She built her own team and paved the way for other women to take part in car racing events.

Dale Earnhardt (1951–2001)

Dale Earnhardt was born in Kannapolis, North Carolina. His father was well-known racecar driver Ralph Earnhardt. Following in his father's footsteps, Dale began racing at the age of 15. From his first season in the NASCAR cup series, Dale was a winning driver. He had a total of 76 wins, which earned him $41,538,362. Dale was the all-time winner at the Daytona International Speedway, and he won the National Motorsports Press Association's Driver of the Year Award. In 2001, Dale died in a crash during the last lap of the Daytona 500.

Jeff Gordon (1971–)

Jeff Gordon was born in Vallejo, California. When he was five years old, his father bought him a midget racecar. Jeff soon showed a talent for racing. By the time he graduated from high school, he had won more than 100 races. In 1992, Jeff raced for the first time in the NASCAR cup series. Over his career, he has had many major wins. A winner of four cup series championships, Jeff has a total of 80 cup series wins. Jeff won the South 500s four times in a row. In 1995 and 1997, Jeff was named Driver of the Year.

Lyn St. James (1947–)

Lyn St. James was born in Willoughby, Ohio. Lyn was interested in sports from an early age. She became involved in drag racing when she was a teenager. After attending the Indy 500 in 1969, her interest in cars and racing grew. She was soon racing them herself. Over the course of her career, she set many firsts for women racers. She was the first woman to average more than 200 miles (322 km) per hour on an oval track. She was also the first woman to win a North American professional road race while driving solo. In 1993, she became the first woman to receive Indianapolis 500 Rookie of the Year honors. Lyn retired from racing in 2001.

Safety First

Racecar drivers are professionals. They work hard to learn the skills needed to drive cars at high speeds. They also use special equipment to help keep them safe. Drivers wear a fire-resistant, one-piece suit. The suit must let the driver move easily enough to steer and climb out of the car quickly in the case of an emergency. Drivers wear helmets that are fitted with special monitors to ensure they do not breathe in harmful fumes from the engine. Seatbelts are made from tightly woven fabrics that do not stretch as much as those in passenger cars. The seatbelts are fitted to each driver.

Influences

Even though Danica's father raced snowmobiles and other vehicles, Danica did not begin racing herself until her sister introduced her to go-kart racing. In no time, Danica developed a passion for the sport. She and her family traveled around the Midwest throughout her childhood so Danica could attend races.

Her family's support has always meant much to Danica, and she believes her success is due in large part to their constant encouragement. Danica's father brought her up to never be satisfied with second place and to always believe she can do better.

■ Tony Stewart won his first racing championship, in go-karting, when he was only eight years old.

Danica has received support from several other drivers. When she was still a young driver, she came to the attention of Lyn St. James. Danica was a guest of Lyn's at the 1997 Indy 500. Danica also mentions Tony Stewart as a strong influence in her racing career. Tony has raced almost every type of racecar, and has won several championships over the course of his career. In 2008, he became the part-owner of a NASCAR team. Danica became a member of this team in 2012.

DANICA'S FAMILY

Danica has been married to Paul Hospenthal since 2005. The couple lives in Phoenix, Arizona. Paul is a physiotherapist. He helps people who have injured their bodies or have problems moving. Paul met Danica when she was referred to him for treatment.

■ Danica met Paul Hospenthal when she sought help for a hip injury she received while doing yoga.

Overcoming Obstacles

Ever since the sport of car racing began, it has been a sport that is dominated and governed by men. "Gentlemen, start your engines" has long been the phrase that officially launches a car race. Women drivers, such as Danica, have had to work hard to prove that women can be successful racecar drivers.

Danica entered racing at an early age. With the help of her parents, she was able to find training opportunities that helped her improve as a driver. Over time, her training and practice showed that she could race just as well as, and sometimes better than, the male drivers. Danica has stayed focused on being a driver and learning the skills needed to improve her driving technique. She has not let traditional **stereotypes** block her from what she wants to do.

■ Other drivers respect Danica's knowledge and skill on the racing circuit.

All racecar drivers face the risks that come with the sport, such as serious injury and even death. It is dangerous to drive a car at very high speeds on a track that is crowded with other cars. Everyone on that track is trying to win the race. Some will make aggressive moves to get an edge over the competition. Sometimes, there are accidents at races. They can be very frightening for the drivers involved.

Danica is very aware of the dangers that come with her job. She accepts that she could be involved in a serious crash. Danica tries to drive as safely as she can to avoid accidents. When track safety is an issue, she registers her concerns with race officials so that improvements and corrections can be made.

■ Racecars travel close to one another on the track. Sometimes, collisions cannot be avoided.

Achievements and Successes

Danica's successes began early in her career. In her first year of professional racing, she won **pole position** three times. This means she had the best times in practice races prior to the main event. As a result of this accomplishment, Danica tied with another racer for the most pole positions earned in a rookie season.

Besides winning Rookie of the Year at the Indianapolis 500, Danica was also named the 2005 IndyCar Rookie of the Year. This meant she had the most racing points of any rookie in the IndyCar racing circuit. From 2005 to 2010, Danica won the title for IndyCar's Most Popular Driver. Since she started racing in the NASCAR series, Danica has achieved three top 10 finishes.

■ Danica is the only woman to have ever led laps in the Indianapolis 500.

Danica's success has earned her recognition beyond the racing world as well. In 2006, after a successful racing year, Danica was named the March of Dimes Sportswoman of the Year. She received the award for her dedication to her career. At the 2008 Kids' Choice Awards, she was voted Favorite Female Athlete.

HELPING OTHERS

Often, celebrities use their popularity to increase public awareness of various issues. They may bring attention to nonprofit organizations, environmental causes, or help fund special causes. Danica has a range of interests that she wants to support. To do this, she has created the Danica Patrick Foundation. The foundation focuses mainly on health-related issues. Over the years, it has supported the G&P Foundation for Cancer Research and the COPD Foundation, which helps people with chronic obstructive pulmonary disease. This is a life-threatening lung disease.

Write a Biography

A person's life story can be the subject of a book. This kind of book is called a biography. Biographies describe the lives of remarkable people, such as those who have achieved great success or have done important things to help others. These people may be alive today, or they may have lived many years ago. Reading a biography can help you learn more about a remarkable person.

At school, you might be asked to write a biography. First, decide who you want to write about. You can choose a racecar driver, such as Danica Patrick, or any other person. Then, find out if your library has any books about this person. Learn as much as you can about him or her. Write down the key events in this person's life. What was this person's childhood like? What has he or she accomplished? What are his or her goals? What makes this person special or unusual?

A concept web is a useful research tool. Read the questions in the following concept web. Answer the questions in your notebook. Your answers will help you write a biography.

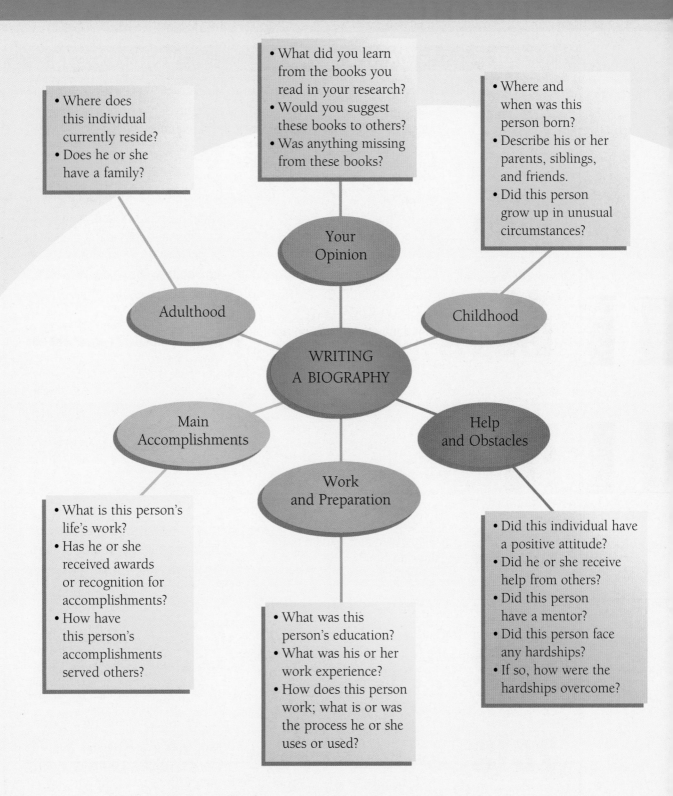

- Where does this individual currently reside?
- Does he or she have a family?

- What did you learn from the books you read in your research?
- Would you suggest these books to others?
- Was anything missing from these books?

- Where and when was this person born?
- Describe his or her parents, siblings, and friends.
- Did this person grow up in unusual circumstances?

Your Opinion

Adulthood

Childhood

WRITING A BIOGRAPHY

Main Accomplishments

Help and Obstacles

Work and Preparation

- What is this person's life's work?
- Has he or she received awards or recognition for accomplishments?
- How have this person's accomplishments served others?

- What was this person's education?
- What was his or her work experience?
- How does this person work; what is or was the process he or she uses or used?

- Did this individual have a positive attitude?
- Did he or she receive help from others?
- Did this person have a mentor?
- Did this person face any hardships?
- If so, how were the hardships overcome?

Timeline

YEAR	DANICA PATRICK	WORLD EVENTS
1982	Danica Patrick is born on March 25.	Gordon Johncock wins the 66th Indianapolis 500 by just 0.16 of a second.
1992	Danica starts racing go-karts.	The final World Sportscar Championship race is held. The series had been one of two major world circuit motor racing championships since the 1950s.
1996	Danica moves to England to focus on her racing.	The Indy Racing League is formed.
2005	Danica starts racing professionally.	Tony Stewart wins the NASCAR championship, his second in four years.
2005	Danica wins the Rookie of the Year title.	Dan Wheldon wins six races in 2005, setting the record for the most victories in a season.
2008	Danica wins the Indy Japan 300, the first female ever to win a major closed-course motorsports race.	Jimmie Johnson wins the NASCAR Cup Series title, his third in a row.
2010	Danica starts driving for NASCAR.	Sony releases the video game Gran Turismo 5 for PlayStation 3.

Key Words

development deal: an arrangement that sees a company agree to train someone in a field if the person agrees to work for the company

drag racing: a competition in which vehicles compete to be the first to cross a set finish line, usually from a standing start

Formula One: the top class of professional motor racing

IndyCar: a single-seat open-cockpit racing car with the engine in the rear, also a type of car racing in which the cars race on a track that slopes

lapped: passed a driver by the length of a full trip around the course

motocross: racing with motorcycles or all-terrain vehicles on unsurfaced roads or tracks

NASCAR: National Association for Stock Car Auto Racing, the organizational body that oversees stock car racing

open-wheeled: cars that have the wheels set away from the body

pole position: the best starting position of the race, on the inside of the track in the first row

precision: the quality, condition, or fact of being exact and accurate

professionally: to do something as a career

rookie: an athlete playing his or her first season for a sports team

scouting: observing and evaluating people to assess their talent

series: a number of car races coming one after another

stereotypes: widely held beliefs that create a certain image of a person or thing

Index

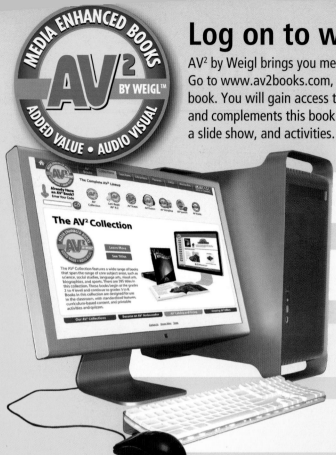

Log on to www.av2books.com

AV² by Weigl brings you media enhanced books that support active learning. Go to www.av2books.com, and enter the special code found on page 2 of this book. You will gain access to enriched and enhanced content that supplements and complements this book. Content includes video, audio, web links, quizzes, a slide show, and activities.

Audio
Listen to sections of the book read aloud.

Video
Watch informative video clips.

Embedded Weblinks
Gain additional information for research.

Try This!
Complete activities and hands-on experiments.

WHAT'S ONLINE?

 Try This!

Complete an activity about your childhood.

Try this activity about key events.

Complete an activity about overcoming obstacles.

Write a biography.

Try this timeline activity.

 Embedded Weblinks

Learn more about Danica Patrick's life.

Learn more about Danica Patrick's achievements.

Check out this site about Danica Patrick.

 Video

Watch a video about Danica Patrick.

Check out another video about Danica Patrick.

EXTRA FEATURES

 Audio
Listen to sections of the book read aloud.

 Key Words
Study vocabulary, and complete a matching word activity.

 Slide Show
View images and captions, and prepare a presentation.

 Quizzes
Test your knowledge.

AV² was built to bridge the gap between print and digital. We encourage you to tell us what you like and what you want to see in the future.
Sign up to be an AV² Ambassador at www.av2books.com/ambassador.